S0-CPF-013

Joy

A Special Gift

To

_____

From

_____

Date

_____

Illustration & Text Copyright © 2001
Kimberly Montgomery

Brownlow Corporation
6309 Airport Freeway
Fort Worth, Texas 76117

All rights reserved.

The use or reprinting of any part
of this book without permission
of the publisher is prohibited.

ISBN 1-57051-951-X

Printed in USA

Tickled Pink

Getting Cozy at Home

Kimberly Montgomery

Brownlow

Welcome

CUDDLE UP

live, laugh, love ♡

The greatest of these is Love. 1 CORINTHIANS 13:13

I'm so tickled to share with you
A cuddly, cozy thought or two,
Ideas for a tasty treat
A yummy meal, happy feet,
Please enjoy this book
It's all for you~
And may it bring a smile
Before you're through!

When you relax? do it with style!

Cut a 'V' in the neck of your sweatshirt to make it easier to get on & off.

Life just gets better with a great pair of FUZZY SLIPPERS!

Evening Attire

Cutie Patootie

A new pair of soft cozy socks will make your feet very happy♡

Sweat pants with open legs are less binding~ more comfy

Super Star

THE PERFECT OUTFIT FOR EATING ICE CREAM OUT OF THE CARTON!

Don't pass up an opportunity to treat yourself really well. ♡

Give yourself the giggles by adding pearls (fake are great!) and fancy slippers to a tank top & boxer ensemble.

TEE HEE
HEE HEE
TEE HEE

NEVER UNDERESTIMATE THE POWER OF A Nap.

THE LEADING CAUSE OF DEATH AMONG FASHION MODELS IS FALLING THROUGH STREET GRATES.
~ Dave Barry ~

Walk the dog everyday,
whether you have one or not!

- Plant some flowers
- Find a swing and get on it
- Gaze at the stars
- Water something

Every good and perfect gift is from above,
coming down from the Father. JAMES 1:17

Prune a rose bush

Gather pinecones

Eat outdoors

Put your feet in a stream

Lay in a hammock

Love one another
deeply from the heart.
1 PETER 1:22

LOVELAND, CO

Suzy Cue
4 Smiling Way
Happy Town
USA

My daughters' 1ST grade
teacher, Mrs. Love (no kidding), sent
Valentines from Loveland to the whole
class. The cards looked so cute and the
kids were, of course, TICKLED PINK!

Sent with Love

Treat someone special to a Valentine from Loveland. The Chamber of Commerce in Loveland, Colorado, has a wonderful re-mailing program that will make your Valentine greeting unique. Here's how:

Enclose your pre-stamped, pre-addressed Valentine in a larger 1st class envelope and mail it to:

Postmaster
ATTN: Valentines
USPS
Loveland, CO 80538-9998

They will handstamp your Valentine with the Loveland cachet, then cancel it with the Loveland postmark and send it off looking special!

FOR MORE INFO, GO TO WWW.INFO@LOVELAND.ORG

Fiddle Dee Dee

I make a lot of mistakes. I don't know why — especially since I spend a lot of time trying **NOT** to make mistakes. However, one thing I have learned is to not bang my head against the wall when I've committed yet another blunder. I do something that feels good. What a concept, huh?

Blunder Control

- A hot bath always helps. So does chocolate.

- Wait a few days. You and a friend will be laughing over it.

- Forgive yourself.

- Think how much wiser you are this year than you were last year.

- Get a pedicure. It's hard to feel totally inept when your feet look great.

Why make the same mistake twice? There are so many new ones to try!

❧ Slice apples and sauté in butter. Sprinkle with cinnamon and sugar and serve over vanilla ice cream.

❧ Add a touch of almond extract to a fresh banana milkshake for a tasty treat.

❧ Cinnamon toast and a cold glass of milk make a cozy bedtime snack.

❧ Warm milk with a few drops of vanilla and a spoonful of sugar is delicious.

French bread and Chocolate

Here's a unique treat traditionally served as an afternoon snack to school children in France.

Simply cut a few slices of French bread and pair it with pieces of your favorite chocolate. You can also melt the chocolate and use it to dip torn pieces of bread in. For an added treat serve it with slices of a favorite fruit.

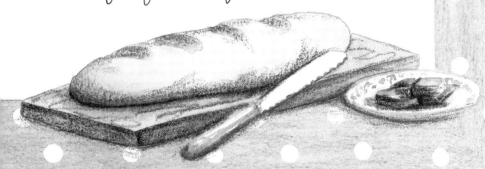

Breakfast for Dinner

For a cozy change of pace try breakfast for dinner. It will warm up your tummy & make you feel good all under! Put on your robe or PJ's, pop in a good movie, & enjoy a comfy nite! ♥

Here's a delicious treat to enjoy with your meal:

Mexican Hot Chocolate

6 c. milk
3 oz. Mexican Chocolate ← Mexican chocolate can be found in the Mexican foods section of the grocery store. Ibarra©, made in Jalisco, is excellent!
1 tsp. cinnamon
3 eggs, beaten

Bring milk to a boil in top of a double boiler. Remove from heat and slowly add chocolate and cinnamon while beating with a whisk. Return to a low boil. Slowly add eggs while whipping constantly. Mixture is ready when thoroughly blended and frothing.

Serves 6.

HOME SWEET HOME ♡ HOME IS WHERE THE HEART IS. 🌸

IT'S SO GOOD TO BE HOME ♪

God blesses the home of the righteous. PROVERBS 3:33

Home is what catches you when you fall ♡

LOTS O' CHOCOLATE

Be Happy

It's one way of being wise.

~Colette~

The LORD has done great things for us, and we are filled with joy. PSALM 126:3

Some pursue happiness, others create it ♥

Vacation Day

Plan an entire day of your favorite activities. Eat breakfast out, visit a local gallery, shop in your favorite stores, meet a friend for lunch, have a pedicure or massage. Whatever your choices make sure they're things you enjoy and the whole day is devoted to

Fun!

October 9
VACATION DAY!
8:00
9:00 Breakfast @ Bernardos
10:00 Gallery Beck w/ Alice
11:00
12:00 lunch w/ Betty

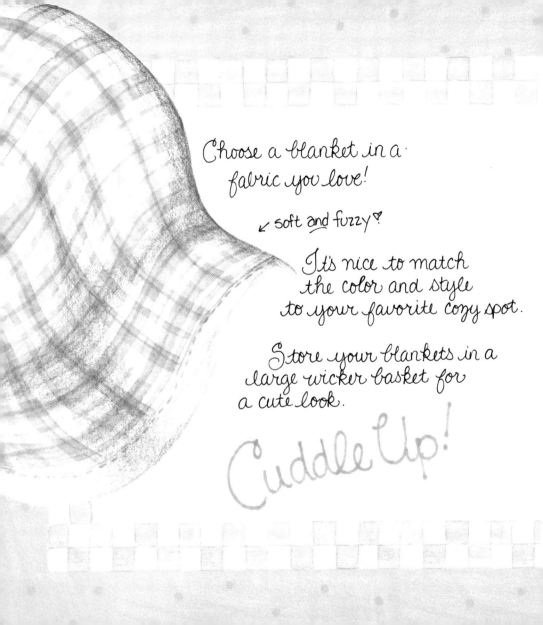

Choose a blanket in a fabric you love!

← soft and fuzzy♡

It's nice to match the color and style to your favorite cozy spot.

Store your blankets in a large wicker basket for a cute look.

Cuddle Up!

A Favorite Blankie

No need to give up a favorite blankie as we grow taller. Grown-ups need comfort too! A soft cuddly blanket feels so good when you need a little pampering. Treat yourself to this little luxury and see what a pleasure it is to come home to. After all, a gazillion babies can't be wrong!

Once you've found the perfect blanket it's time to start searching for just the right Teddy Bear!

It's not how much we have,
but how much we enjoy that makes happiness.
~Spurgeon~

Candles flicker as the bath oil foams,
water scented with fresh cologne.
A fluffy robe hangs on a hook,
fresh flowers give a special look.
The day is done, cares are few,
there's only one thing left to do.
Into the warmth at last I sink,
oh, what joy ~ I'm Tickled Pink!

A happy heart makes the face cheerful.
PROVERBS 15:13

Inside of a dog its too dark to read. ∞ Groucho Marx ∞

Outside of a dog, a book is man's best friend.

We should read
to give our souls
a chance
to luxuriate.

∞ Henry Miller ∞

A Wonderful Story

A Wonderful Story

A Good Book

Reading is a wonderful way to spend a day ~ or a few minutes. Cozying up with a good book can feel like a visit with a treasured friend.

Look for a used book store in your neighborhood. They're a great way to keep your book supply full ~ and the people who work there are generally very helpful♡

Carry a paperback in your purse at all times. You never know when you can turn a long wait into reading time!

TO MAKE NOTES IN YOUR BOOKS ~ YOU'LL ENJOY READING WHAT YOU WROTE IN THE YEARS TO COME ♡

— DON'T BE AFRAID

Tea & Cookies

A cup of hot tea is wonderful. A cup of hot tea with cookies is even better.

Take a few minutes for yourself and enjoy this treat!

Serve one another in love.

GALATIANS 5:13

Tea with crumpets, tea with toast,

Sugar Cookies

2¾ c. flour
1 tsp. baking soda
1½ c. sugar

1 c. butter, softened
1 egg
1 tsp. vanilla extract

1. Preheat oven to 375°.
2. In a small bowl combine flour, baking soda, and baking powder.
3. In a big bowl cream butter and sugar. Beat in egg and vanilla.
4. Slowly beat in flour mixture.
5. Roll teaspoon of dough into balls, place on ungreased cookie sheets. Bake 8-10 minutes. Let cool 2 minutes. Remove and cool.

Yummy!

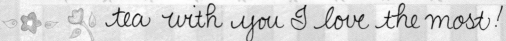 tea with you I love the most!

Happiness,

like good soup,
is always
homemade.

~KAREN'S~ Yummy Lentil Soup

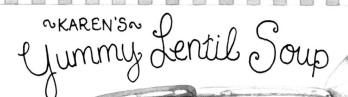

2 c. water
½ c. uncooked brown rice
½ c. dried lentils, rinsed & drained
1 medium onion, chopped
½ c. sliced celery
½ c. diced carrots
¼ c. snipped fresh parsley
1 tsp. oregano
1 large clove garlic, minced
1 bay leaf
3 c. chicken broth
1 14½ oz. tomatoes, undrained
1 T. cider vinegar

Combine all ingredients in a large pot or dutch oven. Bring to a boil, reduce heat, and simmer uncovered 55 minutes to 1 hour, stirring occasionally. Remove bay leaf and serve.

Serves 6-8.

The Sweet Life

Here's one of my favorite treats. Try it with a cold glass of milk! ♡

Pineapple Upside Down Cake

3/4 c. butter, melted
1 1/2 c. brown sugar
20 oz. pineapple rings in juice, sliced in half
1 1/2 c. flour
1 tsp. baking powder
1/4 tsp. salt
5 eggs separated
1 1/2 c. sugar
8 T. pineapple juice

Preheat oven to 375°. Combine melted butter and brown sugar in 13"x9" pan. Arrange pineapple slices in bottom of pan and set aside. Beat egg yolks, then add sugar and juice. Mix together flour, baking powder, and salt, and add to egg mixture. Beat egg white and fold into batter. Pour on top of pineapple slices in pan. Bake 40-45 min. Cool 5 minutes, invert on serving plate and cool completely.

A Healing Gift

An aloe vera plant makes a thoughtful housewarming gift. The lucky new owner can keep the plant on hand for use with everyday ouchies, and as the plant grows so do memories of the home♥

Purchase a small plant at your local nursery. Repot it into a cute container and tie with a ribbon. You may also want to include growing instructions and a list of uses.

How Nice!

PROVERBS 22:9

A generous person will be blessed.

Our happiness is greatest when we contribute most to the happiness of others♥
~Harriet Shepard~

JUST BREAK THE LEAF OPEN
& RUB THE GEL ON.

100% Aloe Vera

You can rub it on burns & cuts.

Try it on a sunburn.

My friend Marta says it's
the best diaper rash treatment!

Fancy Chicken Salad

1 large head Romaine lettuce,
   rinsed and chopped
1 C. sliced celery
4 green onions, chopped
1 can mandarin oranges, drained
1 avocado, chopped
1 apple, chopped
1/4 c. crumbled blue cheese
1/4 c. raisins
1/2 c. candied almonds
   shredded chicken

To Candy Almonds:

Melt 3 T. butter in
non-stick pan. Add sugar,
stirring until melted. Add
almonds and stir until
coated & browned. Turn
onto foil until cooled.

Dressing

1/2 C. vegetable oil
4 T. white wine vinegar
4 T. sugar
2 T. parsley, chopped
1 tsp. salt
1 tsp. pepper

Shake all ingredients
together & pour over salad.

Toss well & serve!

No matter where
I serve my guests
it seems they like
my kitchen best ♡

Plan a 'Friendly Dinner'. Invite a group of good
friends ~ each 'guest' brings the ingredients
for their dish and everyone cooks together ♡
Lots of hands help set the table and clean up.
A fun and easy evening with lots of
time to ENJOY each other.

Practice hospitality.
ROMANS 12:13

The Joy is in the giving!

There's nothing that can give you the warm fuzzies like doing something nice for someone. Imagine if everyday everyone on the planet did at least one thoughtful thing for someone else. What a different world it would be! Giving need not be hard or expensive ~ we're all been blessed by the smallest gesture that seemed so kind. If it made *You* feel loved and special imagine how good the giver felt!

God loves a cheerful giver.

2 CORINTHIANS 9:7

When cooking soup, double the recipe and take half to a friend or neighbor.

A pedicure makes a nice gift for a pregnant friend. Then, when she's in the hospital having the baby, sneak in and clean her house. What a treat for her to come home to!

When you receive a gift that doesn't work for you give it to someone who can use it.

Always pass along a good book.

Call a friend the day before their birthday and tell them how excited you are about the upcoming holiday!

Nobody can do everything, but everyone can do something.

BE RELIEVED OF SOME OF HIS BURDENS. ∞ Ashleigh Brilliant ∞ ♡

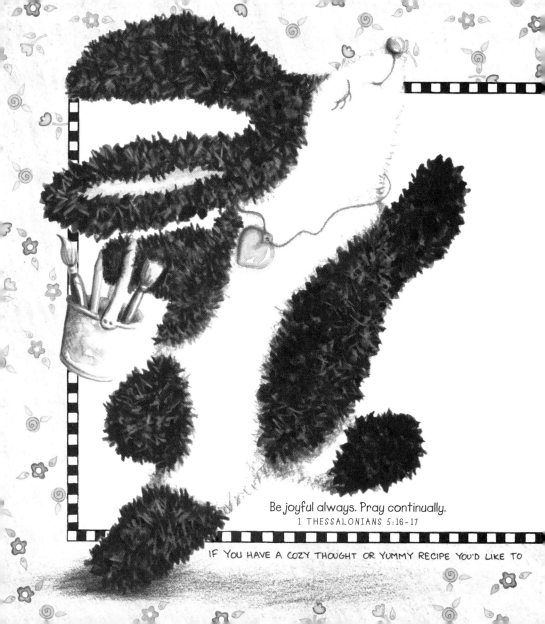

Be joyful always. Pray continually.
1 THESSALONIANS 5:16-17

IF YOU HAVE A COZY THOUGHT OR YUMMY RECIPE YOU'D LIKE TO

Just one more thing before I go...

You deserve the very BEST
in life, in love,
and all the rest.
So treat yourself with
TENDER CARE,
with JOYFUL thoughts,
and lots of PRAYER!
Be well & be happy ~ Kimberly

SHARE I WOULD LOVE TO HEAR FROM YOU! ♥ EMAIL ME AT: KIMBERLYSGARDEN@RCSIS.COM

YOU'LL MAKE MY DAY!